AF375146

# SMART GST FOR SMART ENTREPRENEURS

## A PRACTICAL GUIDE TO AVOID MISTAKES & MAXIMIZE GROWTH

*By*

### ADV. SHYAMAL MODI

# DISCLAIMER

This book is intended solely for educational and informational purposes. It is not a substitute for professional advice, whether legal, financial, or otherwise. While every effort has been made to ensure the accuracy of the information presented, the author and publisher assume no responsibility for any errors, omissions, or outcomes resulting from the use of this information.

Readers are advised to consult with qualified professionals before making any decisions based on the contents of this book. Laws and regulations—especially in taxation and compliance—are subject to frequent changes, and the applicability of rules may vary based on individual circumstances.

The company names, business scenarios, and examples used throughout this book are purely fictional and created for the sole purpose of illustration.

Any resemblance to actual persons, companies, or entities, past or present, is entirely coincidental and unintentional. These examples are designed to reflect common patterns, mistakes, or compliance challenges and are not based on any specific case or client.

No part of this book may be copied, reproduced, stored, transmitted, or distributed in any form—electronic, mechanical, photocopying, recording, or otherwise—without the prior written permission of the author.

By reading this book, you acknowledge that the author and publisher are not liable for any loss or risk, personal or otherwise, incurred as a consequence of the use and application of any content presented herein.

# ABOUT THE AUTHOR

**Adv. Shyamal Modi,** M.Com, LLB, PGDIBO, is a seasoned Tax Advocate and Business Compliance Specialist with over 8 years of experience in guiding startups, SMEs, and emerging entrepreneurs through the landscape of taxation, financial reporting, statutory compliance, and business advisory.

He is the founder of Smart Financial Services, a business consultancy firm that delivers Virtual CFO services to startups and small businesses across India. With a mission to simplify compliance and empower entrepreneurs, he has been instrumental in helping businesses scale, from their inception to sustainable growth.

He is also a certified **Advanced GST Practitioner** from the **MSME Technology Development Centre (PPDC)** run by the Ministry of MSME. He combines technical expertise with a business-first approach, making compliance simple, strategic, and growth-oriented.

Over the years, he has successfully advised a diverse clientele across industries such as **Information Technology, FMCG, Dairy, Restaurants, Retail, Garments, Manpower Services, and more,** catering to a combined turnover exceeding ₹450 Crores. This broad exposure allows him to offer practical insights and industry-specific strategies to each client, making compliance not just a necessity but a competitive edge.

An expert in Income Tax, GST, Financial Reporting, and Personal Finance, he has helped hundreds of businesses navigate complex regulations, avoid costly mistakes, and improve their financial health. His guidance covers a wide spectrum—from **business registrations and statutory filings to budgeting, project financing, and subsidies**.

He is especially passionate about enabling the new generation of digital-first entrepreneurs to operate with confidence. Believing that the future of compliance lies in seamless, technology-driven solutions, he has designed his firm to be fully digital, serving clients remotely across the country with the same efficiency as a local office.

Apart from his consulting work, he is also an active speaker who regularly addresses entrepreneurs and professionals on topics such as tax planning, compliance management, and financial systems for growth. Through webinars, workshops, and knowledge-sharing sessions, he has empowered countless business owners to take charge of their compliance and finances without feeling overwhelmed.

His practical, no-jargon approach to tax and compliance makes him a trusted advisor to businesses that want clarity, peace of mind, and long-term financial success. Whether it's resolving a GST mismatch, structuring a business for tax efficiency, or building systems that scale, he brings a grounded, business-first mindset to every engagement.

This book is a natural extension of his mission—to help new entrepreneurs avoid costly GST mistakes, stay compliant, and focus on what matters most: **growing their business**.

# PREFACE

Starting a business is one of the most exciting journeys you can undertake. You have an idea, a vision, and the determination to build something of your own. But along with this dream comes a heavy dose of responsibility, especially when it comes to complying with the complex and ever-evolving Indian taxation system.

Among all compliance obligations, **GST (Goods and Services Tax)** is one of the most crucial—and confusing—ones for new entrepreneurs. While GST was introduced to unify and simplify indirect taxation, for many businesses, it has become a compliance maze where **a single mistake can snowball into** interest liabilities, penalties, and long-term operational setbacks.

Over the past few years, I've worked closely with hundreds of small business owners, freelancers, manufacturers, service providers, and e-commerce sellers. One thing has become abundantly clear: **it's not the absence of knowledge that causes most GST troubles, but small, unintentional mistakes.** A wrongly selected SAC code, a delayed GSTR filing, an unclaimed ITC, or a missed LUT submission—these may seem minor at first glance, but can lead to major consequences.

That is why I wrote this book.

This is not a textbook. It is not filled with legal definitions or complex interpretations of GST law. Instead, this book is a **practical guide**—a distillation of **real-life GST errors** I've seen businesses make, and more importantly, **how to avoid them.**

**Who is this book for?**

If you're:

- A **new entrepreneur** who has just registered under GST,

- A **freelancer or service provider** figuring out your invoices and returns,

- A **small trader, manufacturer, or e-commerce seller** managing operations and compliance,

- Or even an established business owner who wants to avoid costly slip-ups,

Then this book is for you!

**What Will You Learn?**

Each chapter focuses on a **specific area of GST compliance**—registration, returns, ITC, e-invoicing, e-waybills, export services, job work, and sector-specific errors—and highlights the **most common mistakes** businesses make.

**Here's what makes this book different:**

- It doesn't overwhelm you with rules—it helps you spot and fix what's going wrong.

- It's written in **plain, easy-to-understand language**.

- It uses **practical examples** and tips to show how mistakes happen and what to do instead.

- It covers **sector-specific scenarios**—whether you run a restaurant, an IT firm, a trading business, or a factory.

Throughout the book, you'll see a pattern: many errors stem from **not knowing how GST rules apply to your specific business model** and from a **lack of documentation or delayed, timely action.**

**Why does this matter more today than ever?**

GST compliance is becoming more automated and monitored through interconnected systems—GSTR filings, e-invoicing, e-way bills, ITC matching, and so on. **The margin for error is shrinking.**

What was earlier overlooked may now be flagged by the system automatically. The cost of non-compliance is rising—not just in money but also in wasted time, delayed refunds, damaged credibility, and lost peace of mind. The good news is that **every mistake highlighted in this book is preventable.**

With the right awareness, a few smart systems, and timely action, you can stay compliant and stress-free.

**My promise to you**

This book doesn't claim to cover every technical rule in the GST law. Instead, it **shows you the red flags**—the hidden traps that businesses often overlook. It is designed to be your **reference companion**, something you can return to whenever you are unsure about a decision or a doubt arises.

If this book can help you avoid even one penalty, save one refund from being stuck, or steer your team away from a GST audit nightmare, **it has served its purpose.**

Thank you for picking up this book. I hope it helps you build a profitable, compliant, and future-ready business.

Let's grow your business with clarity and confidence.

**Shyamal Modi**
**May 2025**
*Tax Advocate & Business Consultant*

# ACKNOWLEDGEMENTS

Writing this book has been a deeply fulfilling experience—one that would not have been possible without the unwavering support, guidance, and encouragement of the people who have stood by me in my personal and professional journey.

First and foremost, I would like to express my deepest gratitude to my father, a chartered accountant. From childhood, he has been a guiding light, instilling in me a strong foundation of discipline and integrity. His wisdom and values have been the bedrock of my career. His commitment to professional excellence and ethical practice not only shaped my understanding of the field but also instilled in me the work ethic that defines my practice today. From the very beginning, his guidance has been my compass in navigating the ever-evolving landscape of taxation and compliance.

To my mother, her silent strength and unwavering belief in me have always provided the emotional grounding I needed. Her love, patience, and understanding have been a quiet force behind all my pursuits. She is the calm behind every storm, the comfort behind every risk taken.

To my brother and extended family, thank you for your quiet strength, consistent encouragement, and for always standing by me with trust. Your support gave me the freedom and courage to explore new paths and grow both personally and professionally.

I am especially grateful to my mentors, friends, and colleagues, who have played pivotal roles in shaping my thinking over the years. Through insightful conversations and well-timed questions, you've helped me turn challenges into opportunities. Some lessons came from structured environments, others emerged during long road journeys, and those deeply thoughtful exchanges sparked clarity. In a world full of noise, these moments of shared reflection helped shift perspectives and encouraged growth.

Professionally, I've been fortunate to work alongside peers who value collaboration over competition. Our shared brainstorming sessions—on compliance puzzles, client cases, and innovative solutions—have not only sharpened my skills but deepened my understanding of how to serve those who rely on us better. Together, we've challenged norms, broken through limiting mindsets, and driven better outcomes for those we advise.

A heartfelt thank you to my clients, particularly those from within my extended family and close circle. Many of you placed your trust in me early on, giving me the chance to prove myself. Your belief in my abilities has meant more than any formal endorsement. You've inspired me, challenged me to think differently, and pushed me to explore solutions that extend beyond convention. Your real-world issues and business journeys have played a major role in shaping the chapters of this book.

This book is, in many ways, a reflection of the collective wisdom I've been privileged to witness, absorb, and grow from. Every case, every compliance curveball, and every milestone has contributed to the knowledge and insight I've tried to compile in these pages.

Finally, to you, the reader, thank you for trusting these words. I hope that this book does more than inform. May it guide, empower, and support you in your entrepreneurial journey. May it help you steer your business with more confidence, clarity, and compliance.

**With sincere appreciation,**
**Shyamal Modi**
*Tax Advocate & Business Consultant*

# TABLE OF CONTENTS

# PART A - GST FOUNDATIONS: COMMON MISTAKES EVERY BUSINESS MUST AVOID

# Chapter 1

# REGISTERED, BUT NOT READY: COSTLY GST MISTAKES BUSINESSES MAKE POST-REGISTRATION

Getting your GST registration is an important milestone for your business, and it's commendable if you've done it yourself.

However, many new entrepreneurs stop at just getting the GST number and are not fully aware of the responsibilities that follow. Lack of clarity on what to do next can lead to avoidable mistakes, penalties, or even cancellation of your registration.

To help you stay on the right track, here are some of the most **common mistakes** businesses make after getting their GST registration, and how you can avoid them:

- **Not Displaying the GST Certificate at Business Premises**

Once you receive your GST certificate, it must be displayed at your principal place of business. This is a basic requirement under the GST rules and should not be overlooked.

### ◆ No Display Board with Business & GST Details

It is mandatory to have a display board showing your business name, address, and GST number at your business location. This helps during site verification and builds trust with customers and vendors.

### ◆ Delay in Updating Bank Details on the GST Portal

After your GST registration is approved, you must update your **bank account details on the GST portal within 45 days**. Failing to do so can result in the suspension or **even cancellation of your GST registration**.

Note: If your current account is not ready, you can start by updating a savings account. Once the current account is opened, you can make the necessary changes.

## STARTED YOUR BUSINESS OPERATIONS?

Here are a few more common issues entrepreneurs face after starting operations:

### ◆ Not Providing GST Details While Making Purchases

When you make purchases (goods or services), make sure you provide your GST number to the vendor. If not, the vendor may treat it as a B2C transaction, which means it won't show up in your GSTR-2B. As a result, you might **lose the Input Tax Credit (ITC)**.

If this happens, you can request your vendor to revise the return and mark your invoice as a B2B sale using your GST number.

- **Missing GST Return Filing — Even for NIL Returns**

One common misunderstanding is that if there are no sales in a month, no return needs to be filed. In reality, **return filing is mandatory every month or quarter**, even if there is no business activity.

Not filing on time attracts late fees — even for NIL returns.

- **Not Updating HSN/SAC Codes**

HSN (for goods) and SAC (for services) codes represent the nature of your business activities. Failing to update them correctly on the portal can lead to issues during GST scrutiny or assessments in the future.

## Stay Updated: Managing Business Locations & Records Under GST

Once your GST registration is in place, it's important to keep your business details up to date on the GST portal — especially when it comes to your **business locations** and **record-keeping**.

Let's go through two key areas where entrepreneurs often miss out:

## 1. Not Updating Place of Business Details

Your GST registration must reflect **all the places** from where you operate your business — this includes your main office, warehouses, branch offices, sales offices, etc.

Every such location is known as a **Place of Business**, and it must be declared on the GST portal with proper supporting documents (like a rental agreement, an electricity bill, or ownership proof).

If your principal place of business changes or you **add a new location**, you must **update this on the GST portal within 30 days** by filing an amendment to your registration.

Also remember:

> *If your business expands to another **state**, you must obtain a **separate GST registration** for each state where you are operating. Failing to report your business locations properly can lead to issues during inspections or notices from the department.*

**2. Not Maintaining Sales & Purchase Registers**

As per the GST law, every registered taxpayer is required to maintain basic records, even if they are not required to maintain books of accounts under any other law. This includes:

- A **Sales Register**: A record of all invoices issued during the year.

- A **Purchase Register**: A record of all purchases made for business purposes.

You can maintain these in **physical form** (manual registers) or **electronic format**. If you're not using accounting software to generate invoices, it becomes even more important to maintain a proper list of all your sales and purchase documents manually.

These records not only help you stay compliant but also make it easier to respond in case of any scrutiny or notices from the department.

**Note:**

If you fail to comply with these provisions, the GST officer can impose a **general penalty of up to ₹25,000**.

As a new entrepreneur, it's easy to get caught up in building your business and overlook what comes next. But ignoring your GST responsibilities can cost you in penalties, missed opportunities, cash flow issues, and even the credibility of your business.

The good news? Most of these challenges are preventable with timely action and a little guidance.

Whether it's updating business details, filing returns regularly, or keeping your records in order, every small step adds to your business's financial health and long-term success.

> *Remember, staying compliant isn't just about avoiding penalties — it's about building a trustworthy, growth-ready business.*

# Chapter 2

# MISSING GST DEADLINES: A SMALL DELAY CAN BE A BIG PROBLEM

Many new entrepreneurs believe that missing a GST return deadline is a small issue — something that can be fixed later without much impact.

**However, delayed GST return filing can cause serious trouble for your business**, both financially and legally.

Let's break it down.

Imagine, for some reason, you failed to file your GSTR 1 before the due date. Now you filed it after the 11th of the month. What impact can it have on your business?

- Your customer can't claim the GST credit paid on goods/services taken from you in the same month.

- His cash flow will be impacted for the said month, as he must pay additional GST on his sales and can't claim ITC for the purchases made from you.

- If this happens often with you, the customer will probably switch to another supplier who can provide a regular flow of credit.

- This means you can lose business from your customers.

**Want to Work with Bigger Clients? Your GST Compliance Matters**

As your business grows, you'll naturally want to work with bigger clients, including corporations or well-established businesses. But here's something many new entrepreneurs don't realize:

> *Before doing business with you, most corporate clients check your GST compliance status.*

That's right. They don't just stop at verifying your GST registration — they also check **whether you're filing your GST returns regularly**.

And it's easy for them to find out.

✅ **Anyone who has your GST number can visit the GST portal and see whether you're filing returns on time**.

So if your filings are delayed or missing, it sends a clear message that you may not be serious about compliance, and that can affect your chances of landing big contracts.

**Vendor Onboarding: A Common Step in Big Business Deals**

Large companies have a proper **vendor onboarding process** before they start working with you. During this process, they check:

- If your business is legally registered

- If you have a valid GST registration

- And very importantly, if you're **regular in filing your GST returns**

If they notice that your returns are delayed or frequently missing, they might:

- **Avoid dealing with you altogether**, especially if no agreement is signed yet, because it could affect their Input Tax Credit (ITC).

- Or, if they do go ahead with you, they might **withhold the GST portion** of your invoice until you show proof that you've filed your returns and they've received the ITC.

**This Affects *Your* Cash Flow, Too**

When GST is withheld, you still have to **pay it from your funds first**, wait until the client releases the amount, and only then recover it.

This delays your payments and can create a **cash flow crunch**, especially for small or growing businesses.

**Impact of Raising New Finance for Your Business:**

When you're planning to grow your business, you may look for **new loans, working capital limits, or an increase in your existing credit facilities** (like CC/OD). But here's something you should know:

*Your GST return filing history plays a big role in whether banks will finance your business, and on what terms.*

### 🏦 What Banks Look For

Today, most banks use technology and data to assess risk before lending. When you apply for a loan or credit limit, the bank will:

- Ask for permission to **access your GST data via their API**

- Review your **return filing history.**

- Check the **sales reported in your GST returns.**

- Evaluate how much **tax you're paying**, and whether it matches your declared turnover.

This helps them decide whether you're a reliable borrower and if lending to you is low or high risk.

### ⚠️ What Happens If You're Not Regular with GST Filings?

If banks find that you are often late in filing your returns, or if your GST data shows inconsistency:

- They may **hesitate to approve your loan or credit request**

- You might face **higher interest rates** as a risk buffer.

- They could **reduce or delay the enhancement** of your CC/OD limits

In short, poor GST compliance makes it harder to raise funds, even if your business has potential.

## ☑ A Good Compliance Track Record Builds Financial Credibility

Being **disciplined with GST filing** shows banks that your business is active, transparent, and financially stable. It strengthens your case for getting:

- Quick loan approvals

- Lower interest rates

- Higher credit limits

So, if finance is part of your growth plan, make sure your GST compliance is up to date. It could be the difference between a fast-track loan and a frustrating delay.

**Other Consequences of Late Filing You Shouldn't Ignore:**

### 1. Late Fees – It Adds Up Quickly

- **For GSTR-3B** (monthly summary return): Late fees of ₹**50 per day** (₹25 CGST + ₹25 SGST) are **automatically calculated** when you file your next return.

- **For GSTR-1** (sales return): The same late fee of ₹**50 per day** applies, **but it isn't auto-calculated** — so you're still responsible for paying it, and skipping it could lead to future notices or complications.

## 2. Interest on Late Tax Payment – A Costly Miss

If you delay paying your GST liability, you must pay **interest at 18% per annum** on the **cash portion** (i.e., the amount paid from your funds, not through Input Tax Credit). Here's something to consider:

💡 *The interest you pay on delayed GST is often higher than what banks charge for **CC/OD (Cash Credit/Overdraft)**, which usually ranges from **9% to 13%**.*

So, **using a CC/OD limit to pay GST on time can actually save you money**, compared to paying higher interest later.

## 3. Suspension & Cancellation of GST Registration

This is one of the most serious consequences. If you **fail to file GST returns for six consecutive months**, your registration can be:

- **Suspended automatically** by the department

- **Cancelled** if not resolved in time

Once cancelled, your business can no longer raise GST invoices, claim ITC, or stay legally compliant, and getting it reactivated is a time-consuming process.

**Closing Note:**

Missing a GST deadline may seem like a small oversight at the moment, but as you've seen, its consequences can ripple far beyond a late fee. From strained client relationships and disrupted cash flow to lost opportunities with large buyers and difficulties securing finance, the cost of non-compliance can be significant.

GST is more than just a tax — it's a lens through which your business's credibility is assessed. Clients, lenders, and even potential collaborators look at your filing discipline as a measure of how serious and stable your business truly is.

The good news? This is entirely within your control.

By putting simple systems in place, such as timely bookkeeping, setting calendar reminders, or working with a professional, you can ensure your GST filings stay on track. It's a small habit, but one that builds long-term credibility, financial health, and business readiness.

# Chapter 3

# MISSED INPUT TAX CREDIT? HERE'S WHY GSTR 2A/2B MATCHING MATTERS!

As a business owner, claiming Input Tax Credit (ITC) correctly is crucial to avoid losing out on money. However, many new entrepreneurs overlook the importance of **matching their purchase records** with what's available on the GST portal.

Before we get into the common mistakes made during reconciliation, let's first understand what GSTR 2A, GSTR 2B, and IMS are, and how each one affects your ITC claim.

**What is GSTR 2A?**

GSTR 2A is a **dynamic report**. It shows all your purchases (goods or services) from GST-registered vendors, based on the data they file in their GSTR-1 return.

Let's take an example:

You bought goods from Vendor A on **20th April**. If Vendor A files his GSTR-1 on time (on or before **11th May**), that invoice will appear in your **GSTR 2A for April**.

However, even if your vendor files late, say on 30 **September,** the invoice will **still be reflected in April's GSTR 2A** because that's the actual month of the transaction reported.

Since this report keeps updating whenever vendors file their GSTR-1, it can change anytime, making it harder to track changes or confidently finalize your ITC.

**What is GSTR 2B?**

To solve the confusion caused by GSTR 2A's constant changes, the government introduced **GSTR 2B** — a **static report**. It is generated every month on the **14th** and **does not change after that**.

Using the earlier example again:

If Vendor A files his GSTR-1 of April on **30th September**, that invoice **will not appear in April's GSTR 2B**. Instead, it will be shown in **September's GSTR 2B**.

GSTR 2B helps you clearly see which invoices you can claim ITC on in a particular month, without any surprises or backdated updates.

**What is IMS (Invoice Management System)?**

After using GSTR 2B for a few years, the government noticed a gap:

Taxpayers still couldn't easily track **which invoices they claimed ITC on, which were pending**, or **which were rejected**, especially during audits or while preparing annual returns like GSTR-9 and GSTR-9C.

To fix this, the **Invoice Management System (IMS)** was launched on **14th October 2024**.

With IMS, you can:

- **Accept** an invoice (you're claiming ITC)

- **Reject** an invoice (wrong or not related to your business)

- **Mark as Pending** (you'll claim it later)

With IMS, **you're in control** of your ITC. No more confusion about which invoice was claimed, which one was missed, or why there's a mismatch in the audit.

## How Does GSTR 2A, 2B & IMS Work Together?

Now that you're familiar with what GSTR 2A, 2B, and IMS are, let's see how they work step-by-step when your supplier files their GSTR-1:

1. **First**, when your supplier uploads the sales invoice in their GSTR-1, the data shows up in your **GSTR 2A**.

2. The same invoice also appears in **IMS**, where you can take action on each invoice by marking it as Accept / Reject / Pending.

3. Once you complete your selection in IMS and **submit it**, a fresh **GSTR 2B** is generated.

4. Based on this 2B, your **eligible Input Tax Credit (ITC)** gets **auto-filled** in your monthly return **GSTR 3B**.

⚠ **Important:**

From the **January 2025 return period**, using IMS is **mandatory**. You won't be able to claim ITC unless you go through IMS.

**Quick Comparison: GSTR 2A vs GSTR 2B vs IMS**

| Feature / Use Case | GSTR 2A | IMS | GSTR 2B |
|---|---|---|---|
| **Nature** | Dynamic (keeps changing) | Interactive selection tool | Static (fixed once generated) |
| **When it Updates** | Whenever a vendor files GSTR-1 | Real-time selection once vendor data is available | Generated on the 14th of every month / After updation of IMS |
| **Your Role** | View only | Select invoices (Accept / Reject / Pending) | View the ITC summary based on IMS |
| **Can Be Used to Claim ITC?** | No – for reference only | No – it's for selection purposes only | **Yes – Final report used in 3B** |
| **Auto-filled in GSTR 3B?** | ✕ No | ✕ No | ☑ Yes |
| **Mandatory?** | No | ☑ **Yes** (From Jan 2025) | ☑ Yes |

## Common Issues Faced During ITC Calculation – And How to Solve Them?

Now that you've got a clear understanding of how **GSTR 2A, IMS, and 2B** work, let's look at some **real challenges businesses face** when trying to claim Input Tax Credit (ITC) — and how you can handle them smartly.

Since **IMS is now mandatory**, we'll focus on it while discussing these problems.

### 1. Purchase Made, but Invoices Not Reflecting in IMS

**Scenario:**

You've purchased from a supplier (e.g., Armaanex Ltd.), but the invoice is not appearing in your IMS.

**Possible Reasons:**

- Your GST number was not provided to the supplier.

- Your supplier entered incorrect details, and the invoice was treated as a B2C transaction instead of a B2B transaction.

- The supplier has not filed their GSTR-1 for the relevant period.

**Solution:**

- Ensure your GST details are correctly shared with the supplier.

- Request the supplier to update their records and include your GSTIN in their upcoming GSTR-1 filing.

- Follow up with the supplier to file their return if pending.

**2. Invoices Reflecting in IMS, but the Supplier Has Not Filed GSTR-1**

**Scenario:**

The invoice appears in your IMS because the supplier uploaded the data, but they have not yet submitted their GSTR-1 return.

**Impact:**

- The invoice will not be included in your GSTR 2B until the supplier officially files their return.

- As a result, the ITC cannot be claimed for that invoice in the current period, potentially affecting your working capital.

**Solution:**

- Reach out to the supplier and request prompt filing of their GSTR1.

- Once the return is filed, the invoice will be reflected in your GSTR 2B in the next tax period, allowing you to claim the ITC accordingly.

## 3. Invoices Reflecting in IMS but Not Yet Received from the Supplier

**Scenario:**

You notice that some invoices are visible in your IMS dashboard, but you haven't actually received the invoice document from your supplier yet.

**Why is this a problem?**

As per **Section 16 of the CGST Act**, you can only claim Input Tax Credit (ITC) if you meet **all** of the following conditions:

- You've received the goods or services.

- You have a valid **tax invoice** for the same.

- The invoice is reflected in your **GSTR 2B**.

So, if you haven't received the invoice, even if it's visible in IMS, you **cannot** claim ITC. This is because you are not fulfilling all the legal conditions required to claim ITC.

**When does this usually happen?**

This issue is **common in businesses operating from multiple locations**. For example, if your team at a project site receives goods or services and makes the payment, but forgets to collect and send the invoice to the Head Office (H.O.), the following problems arise:

1.  **ITC was missed** because the invoice was not recorded in your books.

2.  **Expense not recorded** – this can increase your reported profit and tax liability.

3.  **No clarity** – you don't know under which expense head to record the transaction.

**Solution:**

- If your business has multiple locations, **set up a proper internal control system** to ensure that every invoice is submitted to the accounts team or H.O. by the end of the month.

- Request your supplier to **email or courier invoices directly** to the H.O.

- If the invoice details are incorrect in the GST portal, ask the supplier to **amend their GSTR-1** accordingly so the ITC can be claimed without any issues.

**4. Invoices Not Received from the Supplier & Not Getting Reflected in IMS**

**Do you know this can be a serious issue for your business?**

Again, this situation often arises in businesses operating across **multiple locations,** especially when new or untrained staff make purchases either in **cash or by bank transfer** but **fail to collect invoices** or **do not provide the company's GSTIN** to the supplier.

**How Can This Affect Your Business?**

- If payment is made **in cash** and no invoice is collected, **those expenses may never be recorded** in your books.

- If payment is made **through the bank** but invoices are missing, it leads to:

  - Incorrect **creditor balances**.

  - Misstated **accounts payable**.

  - Poor visibility into actual expenses.

As a result:

- **Working capital and cash flow planning are affected.**

- **You may end up paying more income tax** because expenses are underreported, leading to higher declared profits.

**Solution:**

This issue often happens due to a lack of systems and internal checks.

- Create a clear **Standard Operating Procedure (SOP)** to ensure that every payment made by your staff, whether at the branch or project site, is reported to Head Office with proper documentation.

- **Train all new staff** on these SOPs so they understand the importance of collecting invoices and sharing GST details with suppliers.

- Ask suppliers to **send invoices directly to your Head Office**. If the invoice isn't reflected in IMS, request that they **amend their GSTR-1 filing**.

**5. ITC Missed Due to Different Trade Name Displayed in IMS**

Sometimes, businesses miss out on claiming **eligible Input Tax Credits (ITC)** simply because the name reflected in IMS or GSTR-2B **doesn't match the trade name** they're familiar with.

**Here's how this happens:**

Let's say you deal with **ABC & Co.**, a proprietorship firm. You record all purchases under this name in your books. However, when you check the IMS or GSTR-2B report, the entry shows up under the proprietor's **legal name**, say **Mr. A**, instead of **ABC & Co.**

In such cases, you might get confused about the supplier's identity and **skip claiming the ITC** unless you are aware that Mr. A is the proprietor of ABC & Co.

This issue is not limited to proprietorships. Even companies can be hard to identify. For example, one of our restaurant clients saw a purchase entry under the name **Bundl Technologies Pvt. Ltd.**, without realizing that it's the legal name of the popular food delivery brand **Swiggy**.

**Solution:**

- **Always check the GSTIN** mentioned in IMS or GSTR-2 B.

- You can **search the GSTIN on the GST portal** (https://www.gst.gov.in) to find details such as:

  - Legal Name

  - Trade Name

  - Principal Place of Business

  - Locality, etc.

- For popular entities, a quick Google search may also help, but **the GST portal gives the most reliable and verified information**.

Being vigilant about these details ensures you don't **miss out on eligible ITC simply because of** a mismatch in business names.

Missing out on Input Tax Credit isn't just a minor accounting error— it's a direct hit to your profitability and working capital. As we've seen, with the rollout of IMS and the continued importance of GSTR 2A and 2B, the GST system now offers more transparency, but also demands stricter vigilance from taxpayers.

Don't let technology become a hurdle; make it your ally. Set up internal processes, train your team, stay in sync with your suppliers, and review your IMS dashboard regularly. From January 2025 onwards, if you don't take action on invoices in IMS, you won't be able to track invoice-wise ITC claims.

Remember, claiming ITC isn't automatic—it's earned through compliance, coordination, and consistency.

In the next chapter, we'll look at "Blocked Credits under GST" —a crucial topic that explains the scenarios where an ITC, even though reflected in IMS, cannot be used, i.e., must be reversed. Not considering this may lead to costly mistakes and department scrutiny.

# Chapter 4

# BLOCKED CREDITS UNDER GST: AVOID THESE COSTLY MISTAKES

Many new business owners assume that if a bill appears in their GSTR-2B, the **Input Tax Credit (ITC)** is automatically claimable. But that's not the full picture.

Before claiming any ITC, you must ensure that all conditions under **Section 16 of the CGST Act** are satisfied:

- You hold a valid **tax invoice**.

- The **goods or services** have actually been received.

- The goods/services are used **for business purposes** (not personal use).

- The tax has been **paid to the government** by the supplier.

- The item is **not blocked under Section 17(5)**.

Now here comes the surprising part—

You may think that if you are buying a new car to be exclusively used for business and get it billed in the company's name, you can claim the ITC of GST paid (which is 28% of the ex-showroom price).

Even if it is to be used exclusively for your business, you still can't claim ITC if it's a passenger vehicle seating **less than 12 people** (including the driver). The GST paid on such vehicles is **blocked under Section 17(5)**.

The same restriction applies to any **repairs or maintenance** done on such vehicles.

> ✅ ***What you can do instead:*** *You can add the GST amount paid to the vehicle's cost and claim it as depreciation over time in your books.*

**Other Situations Where ITC Is Blocked**

While running a business, you'll come across many expenses that *look* like they should be eligible for GST input credit, but they're **explicitly blocked** under GST law. Here are some key examples:

### 🚫 1. Food & Beverages, Outdoor Catering

Expenses on food, beverages, or catering — even for business meetings or staff — are **not eligible** for ITC.

### 🚫 2. Free Samples Given to Clients

If you distribute **free samples** as part of your marketing, you cannot claim ITC on the cost of those items.

## 🚫 3. Hotel Stay in Another State (Place of Supply Rule)

Let's say you're registered in **Gujarat** and travel to **Mumbai** for a business trip. You stay at a hotel in Mumbai and provide your Gujarat GSTIN.

Since the place of supply is **Maharashtra**, the hotel will charge **CGST + SGST** of Maharashtra, and **you can't claim** that as input credit in Gujarat.

> ✅ ***But if** you travel within Gujarat — say to **Rajkot** — and the hotel charges CGST + SGST of Gujarat, then **ITC is allowed**.*

## 🚫 4. Personal Use or Staff-Related Services

The following expenses are not eligible for ITC, even if paid by the business:

- Life or health insurance

- Medical expenses

- Beauty treatments, cosmetics, or plastic surgeries

- Gym or club memberships (even for employees)

## 🚫 5. Construction of Immovable Property

If you're building a **factory, office, or warehouse** for your use, ITC is **not allowed** on:

- Works contract services (labor, contractors)

- Materials used for construction

## 🚫 6. Non-Resident Taxable Persons

If you're registered as a **non-resident taxable person**, you generally can't claim ITC (with limited exceptions).

## 🚫 7. Lost, Stolen, or Destroyed Goods

If your goods are lost, stolen, or damaged (and not sold), **ITC must be reversed,** or can't be claimed at all.

## Cases Where ITC Looks Blocked but is Actually Allowed

While most personal or vehicle-related expenses are blocked for Input Tax Credit (ITC), there are a few important exceptions that benefit businesses:

### 1. Staff Insurance Mandated by Law

If you're paying for employee health or life insurance because it's *required under any law*, then ITC can be claimed on such premiums.

### 2. Motor Vehicles Used for Training Purposes

If your business provides training services (like a driving school), and you purchase a vehicle for this purpose, then ITC on that vehicle is allowed.

### 3. Trucks and Lorries for Goods Transportation

Purchasing trucks or lorries used to transport goods for your business?

You can claim full ITC on such vehicles — no restrictions apply here.

Understanding blocked credits under GST is crucial to avoid costly errors that could lead to tax demands, interest, or penalties during assessments. While GST law offers input tax credit to ease the burden of cascading taxes, it also clearly defines what's not eligible, especially when it comes to personal use items, passenger vehicles, employee-related perks, and immovable property construction.

As a business owner, never assume eligibility just because the GST is charged or the invoice appears in your GSTR-2B. Always cross-check with Section 17(5) and ensure your purchases genuinely qualify under the law. A small oversight today could become a financial headache tomorrow.

The key takeaway? Be cautious, consult your GST advisor regularly, and develop a practice of verifying ITC eligibility before claiming it, because in GST, not everything that looks claimable actually is.

Ready to move forward? In the next chapter, we'll explore other ITC reversal rules, which, if missed, can lead to a major headache for you later!

# Chapter 5

# ONE MISSED ADJUSTMENT, ONE MAJOR GST MISTAKE: THE HIDDEN DANGERS OF RULES 37, 42 & 43

**Why Timely Payment to Suppliers Matters Under GST**

As you might already know, recently, the Income Tax Act introduced a provision under **Section 43B(h)** to protect MSME suppliers.

It states that if you purchase goods or services from an MSME-registered supplier and do not make the payment within the allowed time limit (usually 15 or 45 days, depending on the agreement), you won't be able to claim that expense while calculating your income tax for that financial year. You can only claim it in the year when the payment is actually made.

Now, a **similar rule exists under the GST law**, known as **Rule 37**. This rule says that if you don't pay your supplier within 180 days from the invoice date, you'll have to reverse the ITC (Input Tax Credit) you had claimed on that purchase, along with interest (if that ITC was already used to pay GST on your sales).

The good part is that once you make the payment, you can reclaim the ITC for the month in which the payment is made.

This is a crucial point that the GST Department checks during audits or scrutiny, so it's important to stay compliant.

**Let's understand this with a simple example:**

- Armaanex Ltd. bought goods worth ₹1,18,000 (including ₹18,000 GST) on credit from XYZ Ltd. in September.

- Armaanex Ltd. claimed the ₹18,000 GST as ITC in the month of purchase.

- However, payment to XYZ Ltd. was made in May the following year, more than 180 days later.

- As per Rule 37, Armaanex Ltd. needs to reverse the ₹18,000 ITC along with interest in the return for the month in which 180 days are crossed.

- Once the payment is made in May, Armaanex Ltd. can reclaim the ₹18,000 ITC in that month's GST return.

**ITC Reversal Under Rule 42 – A Must-Know for Mixed Use of Inputs**

As a business owner, you might sometimes use goods or services for both personal and business purposes, or to make both taxable and exempt supplies.

In such cases, you cannot claim full Input Tax Credit (ITC) on all purchases. Rule 42 of the CGST Rules comes into play here.

**When does Rule 42 apply?**

You need to reverse a portion of ITC if:

- The goods or services are used partly for personal use and partly for business use, or

- They are used to make both **taxable supplies** (including "0% rated supplies") and **exempt supplies**.

**Key points to note:**

- If it's clear that certain inputs are used **only for personal use** or **only for exempt supplies**, then the entire ITC on those inputs must be reversed.

- Supplies that are taxed at 0% (zero-rated), like exports, are still considered *taxable* under GST. They are not "exempt".

**But what if some inputs are used for both business and personal purposes?**

→ In such cases, **5% of that common ITC must be reversed.**

**And if inputs are used for both taxable and exempt supplies?**

→ Then, ITC must be reversed in proportion to your exempt turnover compared to your total turnover.

**Let's look at a practical example:**

**Armaanex Ltd.** buys raw materials worth ₹11,80,000 (including ₹1,80,000 GST) to manufacture two products:

- **Product A** is taxable at 18%

- **Product B** is exempt under GST.

In April, Armaanex Ltd. had a **total turnover of ₹70 lakhs**, ₹50 lakhs of which came from Product A and ₹20 lakhs from Product B.

**How do we calculate ITC reversal?**

- Common ITC = ₹1,80,000

- Exempt turnover = ₹20 lakhs

- Total turnover = ₹70 lakhs

So, ITC to be reversed = ₹1,80,000 × 20 / 70 = ₹51,428.57

Hence, Armaanex Ltd. must reverse ₹51,428.57 under Rule 42.

Many business owners miss this important compliance point—either they're unaware, or they don't inform their tax consultant about the mix of exempt and taxable supplies. This often leads to:

- Incorrect ITC claim

- Department notices

- Interest and penalties

- And most importantly, blocked working capital.

Avoid this costly mistake—review your purchases and their usage regularly and keep your tax advisor informed.

**ITC Reversal Under Rule 43 – Capital Goods Compliance**

Before we dive into the common mistakes, let's first understand what **capital goods** mean under GST:

> *Capital Goods are items you purchase for long-term use in your business and are recorded as fixed assets in your books (not as regular expenses). Examples include machinery, vehicles, furniture, etc.*

Now, let's talk about when **ITC reversal** on capital goods becomes necessary.

**When does Rule 43 apply?**

There are **three main scenarios** where businesses are required to reverse ITC on capital goods, but these are often overlooked:

1. Capital goods are first used for personal use, then later shifted for business use.

2.   Capital goods are first used for exempt supplies and later used for taxable supplies.

3.   Capital goods are used for both taxable and exempt supplies.

Let's break it down:

**For the first two cases:**

If you initially used the capital goods for personal or exempt purposes and then shifted them for business or taxable use, or vice versa, you must reverse the ITC for the time the goods were used for non-business or exempt use.

➡️ The rule: **Reverse ITC at 5% per quarter** (every 3 months) for the duration it was not used for business or taxable purposes.

The useful life of capital goods is assumed to be **5 years (60 months)** from the date of invoice.

**For the third case (most commonly missed):**

When the capital goods are used for both taxable and exempt supplies, you must **reverse the ITC proportionately every month**.

**How?**

Divide the total ITC claimed on capital goods by 60 (months) to get the monthly ITC.

Then, reverse a portion of this monthly ITC based on the ratio of exempt turnover to the total turnover of that particular month.

**Let's understand with an example:**

Continuing with our example of **Armaanex Ltd.**

The company purchased machinery worth ₹50 lakhs + 18% GST = ₹9 lakhs ITC claimed.

This machinery is used to manufacture both taxable (Product A) and exempt (Product B) goods.

**Step 1**: Monthly ITC portion = ₹9,00,000 / 60 = ₹15,000

**Step 2**: In April, sales were:

- ₹50 lakhs (taxable)

- ₹20 lakhs (exempt)

- Total turnover = ₹70 lakhs

**Step 3**: ITC to be reversed for April = ₹15,000 × (20 / 70) = ₹4,285.71

**Why is this important?**

Not reversing ITC when required leads to:

- Interest liability at 18%

- Penalties during assessments or audits

- Reduced credibility with tax authorities

Rules 37, 42, and 43 may sound technical, but they have real financial consequences for your business if ignored. Many businesses unknowingly claim ineligible ITC or forget to reverse it when required, leading to interest demands, penalties, and even frozen working capital.

GST compliance isn't just about filing returns on time. It's about understanding *how your business uses its purchases* — whether they're paid on time, used for personal vs. business purposes, or linked to exempt vs. taxable supplies. These small distinctions make a big difference under GST law.

The key message?

Be proactive, not reactive. Communicate openly with your tax advisor, especially when there are delayed payments, mixed supplies, or capital goods in use. A single missed adjustment under these rules could cost you more than just tax — it could erode your profits, reputation, and compliance track record.

# Chapter 6

# THE COMPOSITION SCHEME TRAP: SMALL TAXPAYERS, BIG MISTAKES

To simplify tax compliance for small businesses, the government introduced the **Composition Scheme under GST**. It offers several benefits, including:

- **Quarterly** tax payment

- Filing only **five returns** per year (Quarterly return-cum-challan and one annual return)

- **Lower tax rates** – Typically 1% for goods and 6% for services (in some cases, 5%)

While the Composition Scheme simplifies compliance, it also comes with **certain restrictions**. Many entrepreneurs are not fully aware of these limitations, leading to costly mistakes. Let's look at some common errors businesses make under this scheme:

## 1. Non-Payment of Reverse Charge (RCM)

One of the most frequent mistakes is **ignoring** the Reverse Charge Mechanism (RCM) liability. Just like regular taxpayers, composite taxpayers must pay GST on specific goods or services availed under RCM at the **applicable rate**.

**Example:**

If you hire a lawyer, GST @ 18% is payable by you under RCM—even if you're under the composition scheme. The catch? You can't claim Input Tax Credit (ITC) on this amount. Failing to pay RCM leads to interest and penalties.

## 2. Selling Through E-Commerce Platforms

Composite taxpayers are not allowed to sell through e-commerce operators. If you're registered under the Composition Scheme, selling through Amazon, Flipkart, Swiggy, or Zomato can violate GST composition rules.

<u>Important for restaurant owners</u>: Selling food via delivery apps also falls under this restriction.

## 3. Making Interstate Sales

A composition dealer can buy from other states but cannot sell outside the state where they're registered.

**Example:**

If Mr. Aditya, a garment trader in Maharashtra, buys goods from Surat (Gujarat), that's fine. But selling those goods in Madhya Pradesh would breach the Composition Scheme rules.

## 4. Issuing Tax Invoices & Charging GST

Composition dealers <u>cannot issue tax invoices or collect GST</u> from customers. They are required to issue a <u>Bill of Supply</u>.

Still, some businesses wrongly:

- Issue tax invoices

- Collect GST at standard rates.

- Do not pass on the ITC to buyers.

This amounts to fraudulent activity under the GST Act and attracts serious penal consequences.

## 5. Not Monitoring Turnover

A critical rule under this scheme is the turnover limit of **Rs. 1.5 crore** per year. Many businesses forget to monitor this.

If your turnover exceeds the threshold:

- You must switch to the regular GST scheme

- Continuing under the composition scheme post-limit is a violation and attracts penalties.

### Penalties for Non-Compliance

If a composition dealer violates the scheme rules, the consequences can be significant:

- General penalty of up to **Rs. 25,000**

- **Compulsory migration** to the regular GST scheme

- Pay tax at **normal rates**, not the concessional ones.

- **Penalty** of up to 100% of the differential tax payable

- **Interest @18%** on unpaid tax

The Composition Scheme was designed to simplify GST for small businesses, but simplicity should not be mistaken for laxity. The scheme comes with strict dos and don'ts, and even unintentional violations can lead to hefty penalties, interest, and forced migration to the regular GST regime.

From unknowingly crossing turnover limits to selling through e-commerce platforms or issuing tax invoices, each misstep under this scheme can have serious consequences. Unfortunately, many small business owners don't realise these errors until they receive a notice from the GST Department.

**The takeaway is clear:**

If you're opting for the Composition Scheme, **stay vigilant, stay informed, and stay within the boundaries**. Regularly monitor your turnover, understand what activities are restricted, and consult a tax advisor before making any significant business move.

# Chapter 7

# RCM IGNORED? YOU'RE SITTING ON A TAX TIME BOMB!

Before diving into this chapter, let's first understand the Reverse Charge Mechanism under GST.

In a regular transaction, the **seller** charges GST on the invoice and pays it to the government.

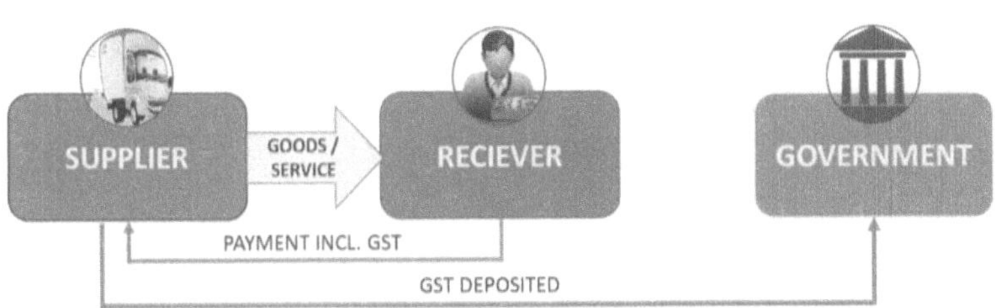



But under RCM, it is just the reverse!

Here, the buyer is responsible for paying GST directly to the government instead of the seller.

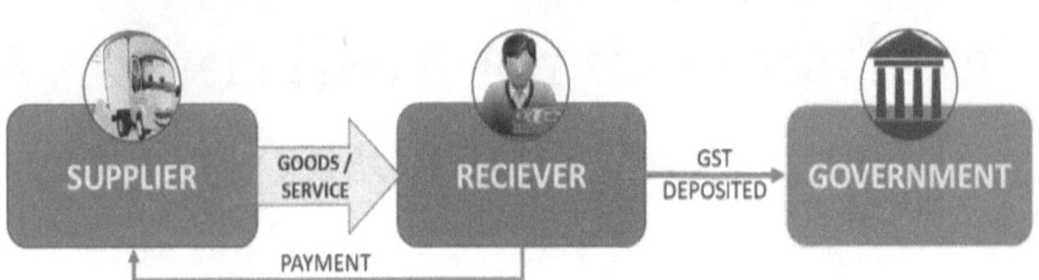



**Busting Common Myths Around RCM:**

✖ **Myth 1: RCM applies to every purchase from an unregistered person**

This is the biggest myth! Yes, this provision existed in the early days of GST, but it was removed very soon.

As the government has noted, RCM applies only to <u>specific goods and services</u>. In some cases, even purchases from <u>registered suppliers</u> may attract RCM.

✖ **Myth 2: RCM adds a huge burden on business owners**

While it's true that <u>RCM must be paid in cash</u> (and not from your ITC balance), the good part is:

👉 You can claim Input Tax Credit (ITC) on it in the same month, subject to certain conditions.

So, if managed properly, RCM won't hurt your cash flow much.

## ✖ Myth 3: RCM is only for large businesses

Many small businesses believe that RCM is not of concern to them. But this is risky thinking. There is no correlation between the RCM provisions and your firm's turnover.

If you take services like legal advice, transport, security, etc., RCM could apply—even if your turnover is small.

Ignoring it can lead to interest, penalties, and even notices from the department.

### 📝 Pro Tip:

Want the **latest list** of goods & services where RCM is applicable?

🔢 Check out: www.smartfinserv.in/rcm-under-gst

## Costly Mistakes Businesses Make with the Reverse Charge Mechanism (RCM)

Let's now look at some of the most common and expensive mistakes small businesses make when it comes to RCM:

### ◇ Not Knowing RCM Applies to You

Many small business owners are unaware that they have any RCM liability.

For example, if you're a manufacturer or trader and you hire a Goods Transport Agency (GTA), RCM likely applies to you.

◇ **Not Issuing Self-Invoice**

If you purchase goods or services from an **unregistered supplier**, and RCM applies, then you must issue an invoice yourself.

This is called **self-invoicing** because the supplier is not allowed to issue a tax invoice under GST.

Most businesses skip this step due to a lack of awareness, which raises a red flag during audits.

◇ **Missing ITC Just Because It's Not in GSTR-2B**

This is a very common mistake.

You may pay RCM using your **cash ledger**, but fail to **claim ITC** because it doesn't appear in GSTR-2 B.

👉 But remember: If the supplier is unregistered, the bill will never show up in GSTR-2B.

You are still allowed to claim ITC for RCM in the same month as GST is paid—keep proper documentation.

◊ **Not Knowing ITC Reversal Rules Also Apply to RCM**

Just because you paid GST under RCM doesn't mean you can always claim ITC.

RCM ITC is also subject to reversal if:

- The item falls under **blocked credit** as per Section 17(5) (like personal expenses, etc)

- **Rule 42** (common use for exempt/taxable supplies) also applies to RCM.

So, be cautious and check if you are actually eligible to use that ITC.

## What Happens If You Ignore RCM?

RCM liability is one of the top areas that GST officers check during audits or scrutiny.

If you fail to pay RCM on time:

- *Interest @ 18% will be charged on unpaid tax.*

- *Penalty up to 100% of the unpaid tax may apply.*

- *You may also lose the right to claim ITC if the time limit to avail of it has passed.*

In short, ignoring RCM can cost you heavily.

Reverse Charge Mechanism is not just a technicality—it's a compliance area that can quietly build into a major tax liability if overlooked. Many businesses, especially smaller ones, assume RCM doesn't apply to them, or worse, don't even know it exists in their transactions. But GST law doesn't differentiate between ignorance and intent—non-compliance attracts interest, penalties, and in some cases, the permanent loss of Input Tax Credit.

The key lies in awareness and discipline:

✓ Know when RCM applies

✓ Issue self-invoices when required

✓ Don't rely solely on GSTR-2B for claiming ITC

✓ Be mindful of reversal rules under Section 17 and Rule 42

If you're running a business in India today, understanding and complying with RCM is not optional—it's essential.

# Chapter 8

# E-INVOICING: THE SILENT COMPLIANCE KILLER BUSINESSES OVERLOOK!

If your business has an annual turnover of more than **₹5 crores**, then e-invoicing is mandatory for your B2B transactions. This includes:

- Taxable sales

- Debit notes

- Credit notes

*Note: E-invoicing is not required for exempt supplies.*

**Common and Costly Mistakes in E-Invoicing**

**1. Not Generating E-Invoices When Required**

Failing to generate an e-invoice, even after crossing the turnover limit, is a serious mistake. In such cases:

- Your invoices become **invalid** under GST law.

- Your customers will **not be able to claim ITC** on such invoices.

- A penalty of **₹10,000 or 100% of the tax amount** (whichever is higher) applies **per invoice**.

*Imagine issuing 200 invoices without e-invoicing — that could result in a ₹20 lakh penalty, despite paying the tax!*

This also affects your business credibility — clients may refuse to work with you due to ITC issues.

## 2. Incorrect Details in the E-Invoice

Details like GSTIN, address, HSN code, or tax rate **must be 100% accurate**. If incorrect:

- The e-invoice can't be edited — it can only be cancelled within 24 hours.

- If not cancelled in time, the invoice stands as-is with errors.

- The penalty of up to ₹25,000 may be imposed for incorrect reporting.

*Always double-check invoice details before generating the e-invoice.*

Note: After 24 hours, an e-invoice can only be deleted while filing GSTR 1 in case of discrepancies.

## 3. Making Changes After Generating the E-Invoice

Many times, it is observed that some minor changes are made to the invoice after generating the e-invoice, such as:

a.   Minor change in invoice number

b.   Minor change in any other details of the invoice

If there is a mismatch in the details of the invoice and the e-invoice generated, it can invalidate the e-invoice.

## 4. Missing Technical Requirements

When generating an e-invoice, ensure:

- **Pin codes** of both the seller and delivery location are provided (especially in "Bill to - Ship to" cases).

- **No duplicate invoice numbers** are used. If an e-invoice is cancelled, the same invoice number cannot be reused.

- E-invoice cancellation is only allowed **within 24 hours**.

## 5. New Rule: 30-Day Deadline from April 1, 2025

A new timeline has been introduced:

From **1st April 2025**, every e-invoice must be generated **within 30 days** of the invoice date.

 *Example:*

If you issue an invoice on **1st April 2025**, the e-invoice must be generated by **30th April 2025**. Post this, the portal will **not allow e-invoice generation** for that invoice date.

E-invoicing isn't just a digital upgrade—it's a legal requirement that has the power to invalidate your entire invoice and directly impact your client's ability to claim Input Tax Credit. For businesses crossing the Rs. five crore turnover threshold, ignoring e-invoicing or treating it casually is no longer an option.

Every error—whether it's a delayed generation, mismatched data, or missing fields—can snowball into penalties, lost clients, and reputational damage. And with the new 30-day rule starting April 1, 2025, the compliance window is getting tighter.

Now is the time to upgrade your invoicing systems, train your team, and adopt a zero-error policy. The cost of ignoring e-invoicing is too high.

In the next chapter, we'll decode E-way bill errors, which can halt your deliveries.

# Chapter 9

# E-WAYBILL ERRORS THAT CAN DERAIL YOUR BUSINESS DELIVERIES!

Under GST, the **E-Waybill** is a crucial document required for transporting goods from one location to another. It helps in ensuring the smooth movement of goods and provides key details like the value, type of goods, sender, recipient, and vehicle used for transport.

However, even a small mistake while generating an E-Waybill can result in shipment delays, vehicle detentions, and penalties.

Let's break down some of the **most common errors** entrepreneurs make and why you should avoid them.

### 1. Wrong Invoice Number

Your E-Waybill must mention the correct invoice number. If it's wrong, the E-Waybill becomes invalid. This can lead to the **detention of goods**, even if everything else is correct.

### 2. Incorrect Date

The validity of the E-Waybill begins from the date mentioned in it. If you enter the wrong date by mistake, the E-Waybill could **expire before the goods even start moving**, resulting in unnecessary penalties.

## 3. Wrong Pincode of the Recipient

The E-Waybill uses the **pincode to calculate the distance** and therefore its validity. If you're sending goods to a branch or warehouse different from the GST-registered address, make sure to enter that new PIN code correctly.

📦 For example:

If the delivery location is actually 450 km away, but you mistakenly enter a pincode that's only 150 km away, your E-Waybill will be valid for just 1 day instead of 3. This can cause the E-Waybill to expire mid-transit.

## 4. Mismatch in Goods Description, HSN, and Value

The details of the goods in your E-Waybill must **match** the invoice exactly and the actual goods being shipped. If there's any mismatch in:

- Goods description

- HSN code

- Value of goods

...the officer may **detain the goods**, resulting in delay, penalties, and other costs such as demurrage.

## 5. Incorrect Vehicle Number

If your goods are being transported through a private or hired vehicle, the **vehicle number must be correctly mentioned** in the E-Waybill. If it doesn't match the vehicle actually transporting the goods, you may face questioning or detention unless a valid reason is provided.

*If you're using a transporter*, they are responsible for updating the vehicle number in **Part B** of the E-Waybill.

## 6. Not Generating E-Waybill When Required

E-Waybill generation is **mandatory** if:

- The value of the goods is **Rs. 50,000 or more**, and

- The distance to be traveled is **more than 50 km.**

If you skip generating the E-Waybill, the goods may be seized during transit, leading to **fines and disruption in delivery**.

## ⚠ Penalty for Non-Compliance

If your goods are moved without a valid E-Waybill or with incorrect details, here's what could happen:

- **Penalty**: ₹10,000 or the amount of tax evaded — whichever is higher

- **Seizure**: The goods and the transport vehicle can be **detained or confiscated**

The E-Waybill is just another compliance formality. Still, it is a powerful checkpoint in the GST ecosystem—one that can make or break your business's supply chain.

From an incorrect pincode to a mismatched HSN code or a forgotten vehicle number update, even the smallest mistake can halt your goods mid-journey, invite penalties, and damage customer relationships. In today's fast-paced business world, delivery delays mean lost credibility and lost revenue.

Think of the E-Waybill not as a burden, but as a passport for your goods to move legally and smoothly. Make accuracy your habit, automate where possible, and train your logistics team to treat the E-Waybill as seriously as the invoice itself.

# Chapter 10

# THINK YOU'RE GST COMPLIANT? THESE COMMON BLUNDERS SAY OTHERWISE

While working with various clients, we've observed that many of them unknowingly make small errors in GST compliance. These mistakes may look minor, but they can lead to interest, penalties, and unnecessary complications for the business.

Let's go over the most common areas where such errors happen:

**Common Invoicing Mistakes:**

Many small businesses either use printed bill books, Excel sheets, or billing software without proper setup. This leads to issues with compliance. Here's what to watch out for:

**1. Not Displaying GSTIN & Incomplete Details in Invoice:**

If you are registered under GST—whether regular or composition—you must show your GST number (GSTIN) on **every invoice**. We've seen cases where key details are either missing or incomplete, such as:

- Business address not mentioned properly

- Invoice numbers are not in the proper order.

- No invoice series maintained

- Invoice date missing

- Customer's name & address not mentioned (especially for B2C invoices over ₹50,000)

- "Bill to" and "Ship to" addresses not shown separately (if different)

- Quantity or product/service details are missing.

- GST breakup (CGST/SGST/IGST) not shown

Not following these basics may attract a general penalty of up to **₹25,000** per invoice.

## 2. GST Calculation Errors in Manual Billing:

Manual invoices using pre-printed bill books often contain mistakes in GST amounts or total values. These errors can confuse your buyer, especially if the invoice amount doesn't match what appears in their GSTR-2B (used for ITC).

## 3. Not Mentioning HSN/SAC Codes:

Every invoice must mention the correct **HSN (for goods)** or **SAC (for services)** code.

At least four digits are mandatory, and businesses with higher turnover may need to show six digits. Not mentioning these can also lead to penalties of up to ₹25,000.

## 4. Wrong HSN Code or GST Rate:

If you use the wrong HSN or GST rate, the product may be classified incorrectly. This may cause issues during goods transport (like detainment of goods), and you may have to pay the tax difference, interest, and penalty.

## 5. Missing Customer's GSTIN in B2B Sales:

If your customer is GST-registered, their GSTIN must be mentioned on the invoice. Without it, your invoice will be treated as B2C, and the customer won't get ITC—this can damage your relationship with them.

## 6. Not Resetting Invoice Numbers in the New Financial Year:

One common issue with businesses using manual billing or simple software is forgetting to reset invoice numbers at the beginning of a new financial year. This leads to duplicate invoice numbers, which is something not allowed under GST.

For example, if you issue invoice #238 in April, and later restart from #1 without adjusting previous numbers, you might again issue #238 in January. This duplicate can confuse you, your customer, and the GST system, which rejects duplicate invoice numbers in the same year. Fixing this afterward damages your professional image and requires extra effort.

### Mistake in Reporting B2C Credit Notes

This is a common issue faced by businesses that don't use accounting software for GST filing.

While B2B credit notes are reported in a separate section in the GSTR-1 return, there is no dedicated table for B2C credit notes. Because of this, many businesses either forget to report them or don't know how, and end up paying extra tax.

So, how should you report B2C credit notes?

You need to **deduct the value of B2C credit notes from the B2C sales** in your GSTR-1 return. This helps in lowering your GST liability. However, if there are **no B2C sales in a particular month**, you may be required to show a **negative value** for B2C sales.

**Not Following Rule 86B – 1% Cash Payment Rule**

Rule 86B is a special provision under GST that restricts the **complete use of Input Tax Credit (ITC)** in certain high turnover cases.

If your monthly **taxable turnover** (excluding nil-rated and exempt items) exceeds **₹50 lakhs**, you **cannot use 100% ITC** to pay your GST liability. **At least 1%** of the total GST payable **must be paid in cash** through your electronic cash ledger.

**Why does this mistake happen?**

This usually happens in businesses that:

- They are in their **early growth stage**,

- Have recently **expanded operations**, or

- Have made **large purchases of capital goods** (like machinery), resulting in a high ITC balance.

Business owners assume they can use their entire ITC to pay GST, but ignoring this rule can lead to interest, penalties, and audit issues.

**Let's understand with an example:**

Remember our company, **Armaanex Ltd.?**

In **June**, their total turnover was ₹90 lakhs, with the following product breakup:

- **Product A (Taxable @18%)** – ₹45 lakhs

- **Product B (Zero-rated)** – ₹15 lakhs

- **Product C (Exempt)** – ₹30 lakhs

Even though the total turnover is ₹90 lakhs, **only ₹45 lakhs is taxable**. Since this is **less than ₹50 lakhs**, Rule 86B does **not apply**.

But suppose taxable sales were ₹55 lakhs instead?

Then total GST liability = ₹9.9 lakhs (₹55 lakhs × 18%)

As per Rule 86B, **Armaanex Ltd. must pay at least 1%, ₹9,900,** in **cash**.

**Exceptions to Rule 86B:**

You don't need to follow this 1% rule if **any one** of the following applies:

- You've paid **income tax of ₹1 lakh or more** in each of the **last two financial years.**

- You've received a **GST refund of over ₹1 lakh** in the previous financial year.

- You've already paid over **1% of your total GST** from your cash ledger during the current year.

- You are a **Government department, PSU, local authority, or statutory body**

GST compliance isn't just about filing returns on time — it's about getting the fundamentals right, every single time. As we've seen in this chapter, simple oversights like missing HSN codes, outdated invoice numbers, or misreporting B2C credit notes can snowball into larger problems, including notices, penalties, and unwanted audits.

The key to staying truly compliant lies in awareness, consistency, and the right systems. Don't let manual errors or outdated billing habits compromise your business's credibility and cash flow. Invest in proper accounting tools, educate your staff, and review your GST practices regularly.

Remember: In the eyes of the law, a "small mistake" is still a mistake — and one that can cost you dearly.

# PART B - SECTOR WATCH: INDUSTRY-WISE GST PITFALLS

# Chapter 11

# CLICK, SHIP... AND MISTAKE? COMMON GST BLUNDERS BY E-COMMERCE SELLERS

With the booming growth of the e-commerce industry, many young entrepreneurs are exploring online selling, either full-time or as a side hustle.

However, many of them unknowingly make costly GST-related mistakes that can derail their business.

Let's break down the most common errors made by those selling on platforms like **Amazon, Flipkart, Meesho, Myntra**, and others.

**1. Not Taking Separate GST Registration for Warehouses in Other States**

**GST registration is mandatory if you sell through e-commerce platforms**. Many platforms encourage sellers to store inventory in their warehouses (like Amazon FBA) across various states to speed up delivery.

**But here's the catch**—if the warehouse is in a state different from your GST-registered state, you must obtain a **separate GST registration** for that state and declare the warehouse your place of business.

## 2. Not Adding E-Commerce Warehouse as an Additional Business Location

If you're using an e-commerce warehouse in **the same state** where you're already registered under GST, you don't need a separate GSTIN. However, you **must add the warehouse address** as an **additional place of business** in your GST registration—ideally within **30 days**. This is done through an amendment application. Failing to do so could attract a **general penalty** under GST law.

## 3. Not Issuing Stock Transfer Invoices for Multi-State Operations

If you're storing goods in warehouses across multiple states and have obtained multiple GST registrations, then every time you shift stock from one state to another, you must raise a **stock transfer invoice** with GST along with an **e-way bill**.

**Example:**

Armaanex Ltd. (registered in Gujarat) stores inventory in Amazon warehouses in Delhi, Karnataka, and West Bengal. When stock is transferred from Gujarat to West Bengal, a **proper invoice** should be issued using the **West Bengal GSTIN**, even if Amazon handles the transfer.

Failure to do so may result in:

- Loss of ITC for the recipient GSTIN

- Payment of GST in cash despite having available ITC

- Inventory mismatches in books

## 4. Not Claiming TCS Collected by E-Commerce Platforms

E-commerce platforms deduct **TCS (Tax Collected at Source)** at 1% on every sale. This amount has been deposited with the government and is **available to you as credit**. However, many sellers **forget to claim it** or confuse it with Income Tax TCS/TDS.

You can **claim this TCS** through a separate form on the GST portal—even for previous periods. There's **no late fee** for claiming this, so ensure you're not leaving the money unclaimed.

## 5. Mismatch Between TCS Return & GSTR 3B

The values reported in your GSTR-3B must match the **TCS return filed by the e-commerce operator**. A mismatch (like underreporting your sales) can raise red flags and lead to **notices from GST authorities**. Always reconcile your sales data with the TCS reports.

## 6. Not Issuing Credit Notes for Returned Goods That Are Resellable

Returns are part and parcel of the e-commerce business. If customers return products in **good, resellable condition**, you should **issue a credit note** and report it in your GST return.

This reduces your GST liability and ensures you don't pay tax twice on the same item when it is sold again.

## 7. Not Reversing ITC on Damaged Goods

If the returned goods are **damaged and unsellable**, the GST input tax credit claimed on them must be **reversed** as per **Section 17(5)** of the GST Act. Not doing so may result in **interest and penalties**. Many sellers miss this rule, especially when goods are damaged during shipping or returns.

## 8. Misreporting Global Sales or Not Reporting at all:

Today, selling internationally through e-commerce platforms like Amazon Global, etc., is easier than ever due to fast enrollment and shipment support from them.

Many new entrepreneurs are exporting products to countries like the US, the UK, and more. However, while doing this, two common mistakes are often made:

### a) Mistaking Exports as Exempt Supplies

Exports are treated as **Zero-Rated Supplies** under GST law, not as **Exempt Supplies**.

This is an important difference:

- In **Zero-Rated Supplies**, you do not charge GST (the rate of GST is 0%), but you can still claim full Input Tax Credit (ITC) and even apply for a **refund** of any unused ITC.

- In **Exempt Supplies**, GST is not applicable, but you must **reverse the ITC** you have claimed to the proportion of such exempt sales, which can unnecessarily increase your tax cost.

➡️ If you wrongly report your export sales as exempt supplies, you may lose the benefit of ITC and reduce your profits.

## b) Not Reporting Export Sales at All

Some sellers assume that since exports are not taxed, they don't need to report them in their GST returns.

This is a serious mistake.

If export sales are not reported:

- Your GSTR-3B return will show a lower turnover,

- TCS returns filed by the e-commerce platform will mismatch with your GST records.

- Your turnover in financial books will not match the turnover reflected in the Income Tax portal (Form 26AS, AIS, and TIS).

➡️ A mismatch in turnover can lead to:

- GST notices for under-reporting sales,

- Income Tax scrutiny for reporting differences.

**In summary:**

E-commerce offers unmatched opportunities, but with it comes a unique set of GST responsibilities that many sellers often overlook, often unknowingly. Whether it's forgetting to register for warehouses in other states, missing TCS claims, or mishandling returns, these mistakes can quietly erode your margins and expose you to unnecessary penalties.

GST compliance for online sellers isn't optional—it's essential. As your operations grow, so do the complexities. By proactively understanding these pitfalls and setting up proper processes for inventory, invoicing, and reconciliation, you can safeguard your profits and scale with confidence.

# Chapter 12

# SERVING FOOD, SERVING MISTAKES: COMMON GST ERRORS MADE BY RESTAURANTS

The food and restaurant industry is booming, especially in newly developing areas of cities. Even though this is a well-established business sector, many restaurant owners still make costly mistakes that can seriously harm their business, especially when the competition is already tough.

Let's walk through some common mistakes made by **standalone restaurants**:

**1. Registered under the Composition Scheme but Supplying through Zomato, Swiggy, etc.**

If you are registered under the **Composition Scheme** in GST, you **cannot** sell your food through e-commerce platforms like **Zomato** or **Swiggy**.

These platforms are treated as **e-commerce operators** under the GST law. Supplying goods through them while they are under the Composition Scheme is a violation and can attract a **penalty of up to ₹25,000.**

Before you sign up for these platforms, make sure your GST registration matches your method of selling.

## 2. Claiming Input Tax Credit (ITC) While Charging 5% GST

Standalone restaurants are taxed at **5% GST**, but **without** the benefit of claiming **Input Tax Credit (ITC)** on your purchases (like raw materials, kitchen equipment, etc.).

If you wrongly claim ITC, it can become a serious issue — you may have to **reverse the ITC claimed**, **pay 18% interest**, and **bear penalties** as well.

Always remember: if you are charging 5% GST, **No ITC** benefit is allowed.

## 3. Not Reporting Sales Made Through Zomato, Swiggy, etc.

You might know that when you sell through Zomato or Swiggy, **they are responsible for collecting and paying GST under the Reverse Charge Mechanism (RCM)** — not you.

However, even if you don't pay GST on these sales, **you must still report** these sales in your GST returns.

Such sales must be reported separately in **Table 12 of GSTR-1** (which was added recently).

If you don't report these correctly:

- Your actual sales will look lower than it is.

- There will be a **mismatch** of sales as per your GST returns and your income tax return (ITR).

- You may receive a **notice from the GST department** asking for clarification or demanding additional tax.

**Mistakes Made by Restaurants Inside Hotel Premises**

If you are running a restaurant located inside a hotel, it is very important to understand the GST rules properly. One of the biggest mistakes seen in such cases is charging the **wrong GST rate** on food sales.

If the **actual room rent** charged by the hotel **exceeds ₹7,500 per day**, then the restaurant **must charge 18% GST** on food and beverages, **with the benefit of claiming Input Tax Credit (ITC).**

However, if you are still charging **5% GST** without carefully tracking the room rent, you could land in trouble.

Here's what can happen:

- If at any point during the year the hotel charges more than ₹7,500 per day for rooms, the restaurant is **required to shift to 18% GST** immediately.

- If you continue charging 5% GST even after the hotel room tariff crosses ₹7,500/day, it will be treated as a **short payment of tax**.

Failing to adjust the GST rate on time may cause:

- A **huge liability** for the unpaid tax.

- **Interest at 18% p.a.** on the short-paid amount.

- **Penalty** for non-compliance.

- Loss of opportunity to claim ITC if the correction is not made quickly.

This mistake can result in major financial losses for your restaurant.

**In Short:**

Running a restaurant may seem simple on the surface, but compliance with GST laws requires careful attention to detail. As we have seen, small mistakes — whether in registration, tax rates, reporting, or claiming input credits — can lead to heavy penalties and financial setbacks.

By understanding the GST requirements clearly and keeping proper records, you can avoid unnecessary trouble and grow your restaurant business confidently. Remember, compliance is not just a legal formality— it is a foundation for building a trustworthy and sustainable brand.

# Chapter 13

# JOB WORK BUSINESSES: COMMON GST PITFALLS THAT COULD COST YOU BIG!

While working with businesses offering **Job Work** and **Works Contract** services, we have observed some critical mistakes that can expose them to heavy tax liabilities and reputational risks. Here's a breakdown:

**1. Raising Invoices as per the Previous Contractor's Bills Without Verification:**

When businesses are awarded a new contract, many follow the invoicing pattern of the previous contractor without verifying the applicable GST rules. They neglect to:

- Check the correct **HSN/SAC code** applicable to their specific scope of work.

- Verify the **correct GST rate** that should be charged under the new contract.

This oversight can be costly.

**In one real case**, a contractor continued to bill at **5% GST**, following the old contractor's pattern, while the actual service required **18% GST**.

What could go wrong in such a case?

- They would be liable to pay the **GST shortfall**, along with **18% p.a. interest**.

- A **penalty**—a minimum of Rs. 10,000 or **10% of the tax amount short paid**, whichever is higher—can be imposed.

- If such an instance comes to notice after the contract is ended, the client may **refuse to pay** the differential tax amount, forcing the contractor to bear the entire burden.

- Such proceedings can damage the reputation of the contractor and impact future business opportunities.

**How We Resolved It:**

- We thoroughly **reviewed their work orders** to understand the exact nature of the services provided.

- Identified the **correct HSN code** and **GST rate** as per law.

- I assisted them in raising **debit notes** to recover the GST shortfall.

- Helped them **negotiate and justify** the revised billing with clients using proper legal references.

## 2. Not Claiming ITC on Workman Insurance Premiums

Another common mistake is ignoring the Input Tax Credit (ITC) on insurance premiums paid for workmen.

While **ITC on insurance** is generally **blocked under Section 17(5)** (for life insurance, health insurance, etc.), **there is an important exception**:

If providing insurance to staff is **mandated by any law**, businesses can **rightfully claim ITC** on the insurance premium paid.

Many businesses miss out on claiming these eligible credits, resulting in unnecessary tax costs.

**Closing Note:**

In conclusion, while businesses providing job work and work contract services play a vital role in the economy, overlooking critical compliance details can lead to significant financial penalties and operational disruptions. By ensuring proper invoicing, correct GST rate application, and claiming eligible ITC, entrepreneurs can safeguard their business from unnecessary tax liabilities and reputational risks.

Staying updated on tax regulations and seeking expert advice when needed can help mitigate these common mistakes and foster smoother business operations. Stay diligent, and your business will continue to thrive in an increasingly complex tax environment.

# Chapter 14

# TRADERS BEWARE: CRITICAL ERRORS THAT CAN COST YOUR BUSINESS

Traders and distributors are crucial players in our economy, as they help move goods from manufacturers to retailers in different areas. In this chapter, we'll discuss common mistakes traders, distributors, and stockists make in GST compliance, which can significantly impact their businesses.

## 1. Recording B2B Sales as B2C

Sometimes, businesses mistakenly record B2B sales as B2C because they have not updated the GST number in the customer database. This mistake prevents customers from claiming the Input Tax Credit (ITC) on their purchases.

**Solution:** If this happens, the transaction can be corrected by filing GSTR 1A or by updating it in the GSTR 1 of the next month.

## 2. Not Mentioning the Correct HSN Code (Minimum 4/6 Digits)

Often, businesses fail to mention the full HSN (Harmonized System of Nomenclature) code on invoices or use the wrong HSN code.

If your annual turnover is over Rs. 5 crore, you must mention a 6-digit HSN code, and if your turnover is up to Rs. 5 crore, a 4-digit HSN code is required.

The HSN code identifies the category of goods you're supplying. If the wrong code is mentioned, the tax rate applied may be incorrect, leading to compliance issues.

### 3. Not Paying RCM on Services from Transporters

As discussed earlier, the Reverse Charge Mechanism (RCM) applies to services received from transporters. However, transporters can choose to charge GST under the forward charge system instead.

Traders must ensure that the transporter is registered under GST and raises invoices accordingly.

If the transporter is not registered, RCM liability still arises, and the trader must pay the tax. Sometimes, traders fail to check this and miss paying the RCM tax on time.

### 4. Not Adding Warehouses or Cold Storage as an Additional Place of Business in the GST Portal

Many traders, distributors, and stockists store goods in third-party warehouses or cold storage facilities and supply them to local markets. If these places are used regularly, they must be registered as additional places of business in the GST portal.

When generating e-way bills for shipments, the address of the warehouse or cold storage should be mentioned as the place of origin. If it's not registered properly, it will violate GST regulations.

## 5. Not Reversing ITC on Damaged or Expired Goods

It's common for goods to get damaged during transit. If this happens, traders must reverse the ITC on the damaged goods in proportion to their value. Similarly, ITC should also be reversed for expired goods. Failure to reverse ITC in these situations could lead to compliance issues.

## 6. Failing to Reverse ITC on Free Samples

Traders and distributors often distribute goods as free samples to attract new customers. However, ITC on such goods needs to be reversed because, under section 17(5) of the GST Act, ITC on free samples is blocked. If the ITC has been claimed on such goods, it should be reversed.

## 7. Delayed Payment to Suppliers

If payments to suppliers have been pending for more than 180 days, the ITC claimed on those goods needs to be reversed as per Rule 37. Once the payment is made, the ITC can be claimed again in the month after the payment is settled.

## 8. Not Levying GST on Freight Charges

Many new business owners forget to calculate GST on the freight or shipping charges collected from the buyer, even when using third-party transportation services.

GST at 18% must be charged on these freight charges and should be included in the same bill. The HSN code for these charges should also be mentioned. Failing to do so could result in penalties and interest if it is flagged during an audit.

**In conclusion**:

As traders, distributors, and stockists, understanding and adhering to GST compliance is crucial for smooth operations and long-term success. Avoiding common mistakes like incorrect invoicing, failure to reverse ITC, or not updating business information can help you minimize risks and penalties.

By staying informed, maintaining accurate records, and taking timely actions, you can ensure your business operates efficiently and remains compliant with GST regulations. Remember, small oversights can lead to big financial consequences, so always stay vigilant and proactive in managing your GST obligations.

# Chapter 15

# THE HIDDEN RISKS: GST ERRORS MANUFACTURERS SHOULD NEVER MAKE

The manufacturing sector is one of the pillars of the Indian economy. The government is constantly working to foster development in the sector to boost the economy by providing various benefits and subsidies for new setups.

However, many manufacturing entities also make mistakes in GST compliance, which can cost them huge amounts.

Let's explore some of these mistakes.

## 1. Non-compliance with Anti-Profiteering rules:

The GST Council regularly reviews the market and recommends changes to GST rates on certain products. When GST rates are reduced, businesses are expected to pass on the benefit of the reduction to consumers by lowering prices.

However, some businesses fail to do this and instead increase their profit margins, even though the government's goal is to make products cheaper for consumers.

Let us understand this with an example:

Our company, Armaanex Ltd, has made a big blunder this time!

The company sells Product A, which was taxed at 18% GST. The GST Council decides to reduce the tax rate to 12%. After this change, Armaanex Ltd. should reduce the MRP of Product A to reflect the lower GST rate.

However, Armaanex Ltd. kept the price of its product the same, without making any changes. This allowed the company to make more profit, going against the government's intention to reduce GST rates and give consumers some financial relief.

If a customer complains about this, Armaanex Ltd. would have to pay the excess profit made, along with a 10% penalty on that amount. This can result in significant financial loss and damage to the company's reputation.

To avoid such issues, manufacturers must ensure they pass on the benefits of any GST rate cuts to their customers.

## 2. Not Claiming Refund in Case of Inverted Duty Structure:

Do you know that if the GST rate on your raw materials is higher than the rate on your finished products, you may end up with an excess balance in your Input Tax Credit (ITC) ledger? This excess balance can be refunded periodically, helping you unlock blocked working capital.

Let's look at an example to understand this better. Continuing with the above example of Armaanex Ltd.

In September, Product A's GST rate was reduced from 18% to 12%, but 18% GST was still levied on the raw materials used to manufacture it. Due to this, the company's major sales come from Product A, which accumulates an excess ITC balance.

At the end of March, the company came to know that it had accumulated an ITC balance of Rs. 20 lakhs due to the inverted duty structure.

The company realised that it unnecessarily blocked its working capital by not periodically claiming refunds. To meet its working capital needs, the company utilized a cash credit facility and paid interest @ 11% p.a.

As a result, the company incurred an additional cost of Rs. 1,10,000/— due to the blocked funds over the last six months. If the refunds had been claimed from time to time, the company could have saved this additional interest cost.

**3. Not Reversing ITC on Scrap or Wastage:**

In the manufacturing process, some raw materials inevitably go to waste or are converted into scrap that cannot be used further. Many manufacturers make the common mistake of not reversing the Input Tax Credit (ITC) on these wasted or scrapped materials.

Let's understand this with an example:

Assume a company uses raw materials **X** and **Y** in equal proportions to manufacture **Product A**. After the manufacturing process, the company gets 95% usable product, meaning 5% of the raw materials are wasted and cannot be used further.

According to the rules under section 17(5) of the CGST Act, the company must reverse the ITC on the proportion of raw materials that went into waste. In this case, the waste percentage is 5%. So, if the total ITC on raw materials **X** and **Y** for April was **Rs. 1 lakh**, the company must reverse **Rs. 5,000** (5% of Rs. 1 lakh) as ITC.

The same rule applies to goods damaged during the manufacturing process. If any goods are damaged, the ITC claimed on those goods must also be reversed.

Failing to reverse such ITC can lead to penalties and interest charges from tax authorities, as this is considered non-compliance with the GST rules.

**4. Not Reversing ITC on By-Products Which are Exempt Under GST:**

Let's extend the previous example to explain this concept more clearly:

In the manufacturing process, when raw materials **X** and **Y** are used, 85% of the materials are used to create **Product A**, 10% become a **by-product (Product B)**, and 5% is **waste**.

Now, let's assume:

- Every 1000 kg of raw materials **X** and **Y** will produce:

- **850 kg of Product A** (which is taxable at 18% GST)

- **100 kg of Product B** (which is exempt from GST)

- **50 kgs of waste** (which also requires ITC reversal)

In this case, the **ITC** on raw materials **X** and **Y** must be reversed based on the proportion of the products being produced. So, if the total ITC claimed on the raw materials used in April is **Rs. 1 lakh**, the company will need to reverse **Rs. 15,000** as follows:

- **Rs. 10,000** for the by-product (Product B), which is exempt under GST

- **Rs. 5,000** for the waste, as explained earlier

If the ITC is not reversed accordingly, the company could face penalties and interest charges from tax authorities for non-compliance with GST rules.

## 5. Inadequate documentation:

Proper documentation is essential for every manufacturer to stay compliant with GST regulations and to ensure smooth business operations. Below are some key registers and records every manufacturer should maintain:

- Goods Received Register (Inward)

- Goods Issued for Consumption Register

- Goods Sent Outward Register

- Yield Register showing raw materials (RM) converted into finished goods (FG), by-products, or wastage.

- Lorry Receipts for inward and outward transportation

- Sales and Purchase Invoices

The **Yield Register** is particularly important for two reasons:

1. It helps during **GST department audits** or scrutiny, ensuring that ITC reversal is done accurately.

2. It enables tracking the **actual yield** compared to the **standard yield** in production.

If the GST department challenges any of your transactions and you don't have proper documentation to back them up, they could be seen as bogus transactions. This may result in **hefty penalties** and potential legal complications.

**6. Not reporting Job Work transactions:**

Many businesses outsource certain processes to streamline operations, reduce time, and lower setup costs. For example, some initial processing of raw materials might be outsourced before they are brought back to the factory for further processing.

However, it's essential to report such job work transactions in **Form ITC-04** on a quarterly basis. Failing to do so can lead to several issues:

- **Non-compliance**: Not filing Form ITC-04 can raise red flags with tax authorities, potentially triggering more detailed investigations.

- **Rejection or Reversal of ITC Claims**: Missing documentation for job work transactions may result in tax authorities rejecting or reversing your ITC claims, which could lead to interest liabilities.

**Important Note**: If goods sent for job work are not received back within **12 months** (or **36 months** for capital goods), they may be treated as a sale transaction under GST law.

**In conclusion,**

Manufacturing businesses play a crucial role in the economy, and staying on top of GST compliance is key to avoiding costly mistakes. Small errors, such as not reversing ITC on scrap, failing to report job work transactions, or lacking proper documentation, can lead to penalties and financial losses.

By maintaining accurate records, filing returns on time, and staying informed about GST changes, manufacturers can protect their business from unnecessary risks. Regular checks and updates will help ensure smooth operations and compliance with tax regulations.

# Chapter 16

# HIDDEN GST TRAPS FOR SERVICE BUSINESSES – ARE YOU FALLING INTO THEM?

The service sector is a major contributor to India's economy, with the IT industry booming like never before.

However, many new entrepreneurs unknowingly make GST compliance mistakes that can cost them heavily in penalties and interest.

Let's break down some of the common ones:

## 1. Not Paying GST on Advances Received

If you receive an advance from a client before starting work, you must pay GST on that advance, even if you haven't raised an invoice yet.

Many entrepreneurs skip this step due to a lack of awareness, which leads to interest liabilities and penalties later on.

**Pro Tip:**

Raise a partial invoice for the advance received. This way, the transaction gets properly reported in your GST returns, and your client can also claim Input Tax Credit (ITC) easily.

## 2. Using Incorrect SAC Codes

Just like products have HSN codes, services have SAC (Service Accounting Codes). Many service providers wrongly mention SAC codes on invoices because they believe it doesn't matter if the GST rate (mostly 18%) remains the same.

But here's why it matters:

- <u>Risk of Notices & Penalties</u>:

Mentioning the wrong SAC code on invoices is considered a compliance error. Even though the tax rate might be the same, it can trigger penalties or scrutiny from tax authorities. Imagine having to answer unnecessary queries or pay penalties just because of a code mismatch—it's not worth the headache!

- <u>Impact on Input Tax Credit (ITC)</u>:

Clients claiming ITC based on inaccurate SAC codes risk rejection of ITC claims during verification/scrutiny, which can potentially harm your business relationships with them.

- <u>Complications if Tax Rate Changes</u>:

Today, the GST rate might be the same (18%), but if GST rates are revised in the future, past invoices with incorrect SAC codes could lead to reconciliation problems or retroactive penalties if authorities discover such discrepancies.

- <u>Time and Effort Wasted</u>:

If a mismatch is identified later, you will likely need to amend invoices, returns, or respond to notices, which can be resource-intensive and disruptive.

Always ensure the correct SAC code is used in every invoice.

## 3. Not Filing LUT for Export of Services

If you are providing IT services to overseas clients, you can export services without paying GST by filing a **Letter of Undertaking (LUT)**.

However, many first-time exporters aren't aware of this.

**If you do not file LUT:**

- You must pay 18% GST on your invoices along with interest, causing a cash flow strain.

- You can claim a refund later, but the process is lengthy, requires perfect documentation, and invites heavy scrutiny if errors are found.

**Key Point:**

Always file your LUT **before** raising any export invoice. LUTs are valid for one financial year and must be renewed annually.

## 4. Delayed or Non-Issuance of Invoices

Unlike goods, services do not involve physical movement. Hence, it's your responsibility to issue invoices **within 30 days of completing the service**.

**Tax Liability Arises at the Earliest of:**

- Date of invoice (if issued within 30 days)

- Date of receipt of payment

- Date of service completion (if invoice not issued in time)

In the case of continuous services (like monthly maintenance contracts), the tax liability arises on the date of payment receipt, invoice issuance, or milestone completion, whichever is earlier.

### Tip:

Always issue invoices promptly to avoid unnecessary interest, penalties, and audit issues.

## 5. Not Having Service Contracts or Agreements

A **written service contract or agreement** is crucial. It clearly defines the nature of services, payment terms, timelines, and applicable GST rates/SAC codes.

**Without a service contract:**

- Classifying the service and choosing the correct SAC code becomes difficult.

- Clients may dispute GST charges, leading to payment delays.

- During audits, tax authorities may reject your invoices if there's no supporting agreement.

- Refunds (especially for export services under LUT) might get rejected.

**Advice:**

Always sign a basic service agreement before starting work. It protects you legally and supports your GST compliance.

**Closing Note**

Building a successful service business is not just about delivering great work—it's also about staying sharp with your compliance. By understanding and avoiding these common GST mistakes, you protect your business from unnecessary costs, audits, and hurdles that can slow you down. Remember, every smart step you take towards compliance strengthens your credibility, improves your cash flow, and prepares you for bigger growth opportunities.

Stay proactive, stay compliant, and let your business soar beyond boundaries!

# NAVIGATING THE FUTURE

## MASTERING GST COMPLIANCE FOR BUSINESS SUCCESS

As we conclude this journey through the intricacies of GST compliance, it's important to reflect on the challenges businesses face and the evolving landscape of the GST regime. The GST era has fundamentally transformed the way businesses operate in India, and as we move forward, challenges and opportunities await.

GST compliance is no longer just about ticking boxes on a checklist. It's about building a resilient business that can adapt to evolving tax laws and systems. The common mistakes discussed in this book—ranging from missed deadlines to incorrect invoicing, blocked credits, and misunderstood rules—are real hurdles that can hinder business growth, disrupt cash flow, and lead to unnecessary penalties.

However, these challenges are not insurmountable. With careful planning, awareness, and timely action, businesses can navigate the complexities of GST and turn compliance into a strategic advantage.

The path ahead for businesses lies in adopting a proactive mindset. GST is not a one-time concern but an ongoing responsibility that requires attention to detail, timely action, and a solid understanding of the regulations.

For entrepreneurs and business owners, this means fostering a culture of compliance within their organizations, ensuring that the entire team, from finance to operations, understands their roles in maintaining GST standards.

## The Future of GST: A Dynamic Landscape

As we've seen throughout this book, GST compliance is a vital aspect of running a successful business in today's economy. For entrepreneurs, whether you're just starting or managing an established business, understanding and adhering to GST regulations is key to avoiding costly mistakes and ensuring smooth operations. Here's a look at what lies ahead and how you can master GST compliance for long-term business success:

### 1. GST Compliance is Essential for Business Growth

GST isn't just a tax obligation—it's an integral part of your business operations. From invoicing to filing returns, every step of GST compliance impacts your cash flow, profitability, and overall efficiency. Staying compliant helps you build credibility, avoid penalties, and streamline your processes, which ultimately contributes to your business growth.

### 2. Proactive Management is Key

Staying on top of your GST obligations is crucial for avoiding common mistakes that can escalate into bigger problems. Whether you miss deadlines, overlook input tax credits, or fail to report transactions properly, proactive management ensures you address issues before they turn into costly errors.

### 3. Small Mistakes Can Have Big Consequences

While the mistakes discussed in this book may seem minor at first, their cumulative impact can be significant. From missing input tax credits to not reversing credits on damaged goods, such oversights can lead to penalties, interest, and even disruption in business operations. Attention to detail is crucial to prevent these small errors from growing into larger financial setbacks.

### 4. Technology and Tools Are Your Allies

Embrace technology to simplify GST compliance. Using accounting software and digital tools for invoicing, return filing, and record-keeping can significantly reduce the risk of errors and improve efficiency. Leveraging the latest technology will not only help you stay compliant but also streamline your entire business operation, reducing manual effort and increasing accuracy.

### 5. Adapt to Changes in GST Laws

GST laws and rules are continuously evolving. To stay ahead, keep yourself updated on the latest amendments and notifications. Regularly reviewing and adjusting your processes according to new guidelines will help you avoid surprises and remain compliant in a dynamic environment.

## 6. GST Compliance is a Competitive Advantage

Businesses that master GST compliance gain a competitive edge. By ensuring timely filings, accurate invoicing, and proper reporting, you reduce your risks and improve your credibility with customers, suppliers, and authorities. When your business is compliant, it can operate smoothly, focus on growth, and avoid unnecessary stress.

## 7. Focus on Risk Mitigation

While compliance is essential, so is risk mitigation. Implementing proper checks and balances to avoid common mistakes like missing stock transfer invoices or misreporting export sales will protect you from unnecessary liabilities. Developing strong internal controls and conducting regular internal audits will keep your business in the clear.

## 8. Planning for Future Challenges

The GST journey doesn't stop here. As your business grows and expands, your GST obligations will become more complex. Make sure you plan for future challenges like multi-state operations, e-commerce transactions, and export sales. Staying prepared and building a solid compliance framework from the start will save you time, money, and effort as your business scales.

## 9. Work Closely with Experts

Navigating the complexities of GST requires expertise. Collaborating with tax professionals and consultants who understand the ins and outs of GST will help you stay compliant and make informed decisions. They can also provide valuable advice on managing your GST liability, optimizing cash flow, and addressing any issues that arise.

## 10. Final Thought: A Proactive Approach to GST for Long-Term Success

The key takeaway is this: successful GST compliance is all about being proactive, staying informed, and adapting quickly to changes. By consistently managing your GST obligations, avoiding common mistakes, and leveraging the right tools and expert advice, you're positioning your business for long-term stability and growth.

In conclusion, mastering GST compliance is a continuous journey, but it doesn't have to be overwhelming. Stay vigilant, embrace technology, and keep learning. With the right strategies in place, GST compliance can become one of your business's greatest assets, helping you operate smoothly and efficiently while driving future growth.

# YOUR FEEDBACK MATTERS

Thank you for taking the time to read this book. I hope it offered practical insights that help you avoid costly GST mistakes and operate your business with greater clarity and confidence.

If you found value in this book, I'd be grateful if you could spare just 30 seconds to leave an honest review. Your feedback not only helps improve future editions but also helps other entrepreneurs discover content that could benefit them.

If you spot any errors or have suggestions for improvement, I'd love to hear from you—your input will help make future versions even better.

**Connect with the Author:**

If you have any questions regarding the topics covered in the book, feel free to connect with the author. Want future updates? Join our WhatsApp channel by scanning the QR code below!

**Contact:**

 +91-90333 77645

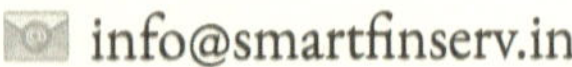 info@smartfinserv.in

🌐 www.smartfinserv.in

www.ingramcontent.com/pod-product-compliance
Lightning Source LLC
Chambersburg PA
CBHW021224130726
47988CB00002B/803